Leadership

Acquiring Expertise In Leadership Skills: Leadership Fundamentals That Can Be Applied In Any Aspect Of Your Life

(The Ultimate Guide To Leading And Influencing Others To Achieve Success)

Kieth Blackburn

TABLE OF CONTENT

The Obligations Or Responsibilities Of The Leader..1

Employee Onboarding, Offboarding, Termination, Resignation, And Layoffs, As Well As Employee Retention..5

Increasing Your Capabilities As A Leader.........18

Activities For The Development Of Leadership 29

Management Of Both Leadership And Time Is Essential. 63

Is It True That Women Have Greater Emotional Intelligence Than Men?...69

It Is Essential To Be Competent. Certainty Is Of The Utmost Importance..81

Enhancing Organizational Productivity Through Higher Emotional Intelligence In Corporations...87

Develop Relationships With Your Staff Members..96

The Leader Who Is Able To Communicate....107

Intellectual Communication Is Essential.........111

The Fights Behind Closed Doors........................122

Acquaint Yourself With The Ideal Methods Of Leadership.. 144

Having A Clear Understanding Of Your Destiny
.... 155

The Obligations Or Responsibilities Of The Leader

The sensation that they are in the right place is one of those messages that might be very challenging for leaders to convey at times. Executives, high-level managers, mid-level managers, and even team leaders have a responsibility to provide some insight into what it is that they need to achieve. Leaders are often required to wear a variety of hats, and within the span of a single day, they may alter the way in which several different rules are applied. As a consequence of this, the members of the team may have the misconception that their role is limited to providing answers or giving approval, and that the leader should be informed of every issue, disagreement, and decision. If a leader fails to convey the tasks associated with their position, there is a good chance that they will be overtaken by others and left alone. You should review this topic on a frequent basis if you want to develop into a leader who can rely on their followers for inspiration and guidance.

When it comes to discussing your responsibilities or the regulations, the most effective way to begin is with brief periods of face-to-face conversation. If your team has a morning huddle or a standing meeting every day, those are the best moments to discuss the things that you need to put your attention on in the days to come. These sessions are an excellent chance to discuss your availability to respond to enquiries and resolve issues as they crop up. For instance, if you are getting close to the end of the quarter and have executive reports to write, financial reports to examine, and the onboarding of new staff at the start of the following month to plan, then it is possible that you will not have much time. When you realize that you have a crowded calendar, it is vital to let your team know that you have things that you need to complete, but at the same time, you should provide them with clear access points. Take advantage of this chance to allocate tasks to team leaders and designate point individuals to field inquiries in areas of expertise for which they are uniquely qualified.

When you have reached the point where it seems like every issue is coming to your desk and that you are the bottleneck, it is time to hold a discussion with the rest of the department. It is great practice to have separate meetings for each team if you are managing a department that has many teams. It may seem to be a more effective use of time to have one department meeting in which everyone attends, but doing so would result in the loss of an essential component of the company's identity and mission.

Because there are fewer people in the room and you've separated the teams, you'll be able to address each team based on the role they play within the division and engage with one another in a more meaningful way. You should take advantage of the fact that these sessions are a chance to reveal that you are aware that you are the bottleneck. You might utilize these sessions as an interactive workshop to determine methods to minimize bottlenecks, provide greater authority when answering queries, or present information to team managers or team leaders in order to develop trust in your team's capabilities.

Employee Onboarding, Offboarding, Termination, Resignation, And Layoffs, As Well As Employee Retention

Every leader in the organization or on your team will have the chance to express messages at extremely significant periods in their careers, either inside the firm or with their respective teams. Onboarding and retention are processes that will be experienced by every employee. It is always an option for employees to quit, and the corporation has the right to implement layoffs or dismiss particular workers. These kind of talks are often challenging for leaders to have.

Although onboarding is the least difficult of these factors, it nonetheless has the potential to aggravate members of a team or lead to misunderstanding. If members of the team sought for a new post or promotion, but an outside party was recruited instead, the leader may feel as if they are placed in a difficult situation. You have the option of commenting on the choice or ignoring it entirely. If this is the case, then you should probably stick to text-based communication in order to establish the tone that this is less of a debate and more of an acknowledgment of their efforts on your part.

An essential point to emphasize is that introducing a new member to the team during the onboarding process does not necessarily need to take place in the form of a meeting.

Termination is a difficult topic to discuss, but it is imperative that it be done so face to face at all times. Take extra care to ensure that you do not engage in any kind of communication that relies on text before the termination takes effect. After then, it may be important to tell the team about the termination, which may also be done by email, a memo, or an update in a messaging service. Depending on the circumstances, this step may or may not be required. There aren't very many valid reasons to call a meeting to talk about firing another worker, but you should do it nevertheless. Theft, serious wrongdoing, or the exploitation of pre-existing regulations are some examples of these justifications.

The problem of layoffs is another complicated and touchy topic that has to be discussed. It's possible that the employee will or won't notice the layoff coming. Even in the case that there will be widespread layoffs, the management team is obligated to take the effort to meet personally with each employee who will be terminated from their position. Do not utilize red slips, email, or any other type of contact to advise someone that they have lost their job as a result of the firm underperforming or downsizing. This includes all other forms of communication as well.

The most beneficial aspects of the issues discussed here are employee resignations and retention rates. It is generally easy to accept a resignation, and in most cases, the employee will take the initiative to notify you in person of their decision to leave. When you get to this fork in the road, you should ask the worker who is leaving for directions. If the worker requests to take a seat and have a chat, you should accommodate their request. It's possible that he or she won't want to discuss it with you if they contact you to let you know that they've given their two-week notice to human resources, in which case you shouldn't bother talking to them about it. If the employee gives their resignation to you through email or text message, you should at the very least make an offer to take part in the departure interview.

Discussions on retention must to take place at regular periods. In most cases, these discussions do not have to take place on a weekly basis; nonetheless, it is possible that they are useful for quarterly, semiannual, or annual performance assessments. It is worthwhile to investigate what it would take to keep an employee on while you are evaluating the influence that the employee's performance has had on the organization. Naturally, you shouldn't directly inquire as to whether or not they are willing to remain in their current location. Instead, steer the discourse toward participation in the activity. Ask straightforward questions about an employee's level of engagement and how they believe they can continue to perform inside the firm during a face-to-face conversation, which should normally take place during a performance review or analysis.

Motivation and Mental Attitude

In 1982, I received my certification to practice as a physiotherapist. My original plan was to pursue a career in medicine, but since I did not put enough effort into my last year of high school, I did not get the grades necessary to go to medical school.

After gaining an insightful understanding of the importance of concentration, I resolved to propel my professional development by securing a position at a famous teaching hospital in London. My frame of mind and my drive enabled me to achieve the aim, which was to begin my professional life at University College Hospital in London.

Almost immediately, I came to the realization that supporting individuals in recovering from illness and injuries was quite satisfying. I was more interested in learning about the factors that contribute to peak human performance.

The absence of sickness or infirmity is not the same thing as being healthy; rather, being healthy refers to a condition of full mental, bodily, and social well-being. (no date given by the World Health Organization)

Because of my natural inquisitiveness, I decided to pursue more education in a variety of fields, such as philosophy, psychology, acupuncture, hypnosis, neuro-linguistic programming (NLP), and neurosemantics.

I left the hospital to work with athletes and sports teams to assist them rehabilitate while also preparing them to compete well in their respective sports. It was obvious that mindset and drive were the X elements that made the difference in both the rate of recuperation and the outcome of the competition.

A person's mentality may be defined as a collection of self-perceptions or ideas that they have about themselves. These are the factors that decide one's actions, perspectives, and mental attitude. The term "motivation" comes from the Latin word "movere," which literally means "to move." The term "motivation" refers to the collection of factors, either external or internal to a person, that are responsible for the stimulation, direction, and maintenance of goal-oriented, voluntary effort.

After graduating from college eighteen years ago, I had just begun my career as a coach and public speaker and was in the process of developing a strategy for self-leadership when I was presented with a lucky opportunity. When I was just starting out as a consultant, money was tight, so to supplement my income, I took a job working as a physiotherapist in the clinic of a fellow professional in North Sydney.

One day, I was treating a patient who complained of having a tight neck. While I stretched and twisted him back into shape, we continued our conversation. He was a young CEO who was attempting to instill a sense of belief in his workforce. I told him some of my thoughts, and he seemed taken aback by them. He told me, "You don't talk like a physiotherapist," and I couldn't disagree more.

After I told him about how I got started in the business of executive coaching, he invited me to his office and said, "Come and see me there." I'm not sure whether I can do this on my own. What happened after that, as the saying goes, is history.

My first CEO client was Grant Halloran, and I assisted him in scaling both himself and his start-up team to the point where they were acquired. Mel Dreuth's desire for a first-time manager's training spurred the creation of the New Leadership Framework and the production of this book. Grant is now the CEO of Planful Inc., and we still work together. This is how I met Mel Dreuth, whose need for a first-time manager's training brought us together.

There are two different mindsets: the fixed mentality and the development mindset, as described by Carol S. Dweck, PhD, in her book mentality: The New Psychology of Success (Dweck, 2007).

When you have a fixed mentality, you feel the need to constantly prove yourself, and you see criticism as a personal assault that has to be avoided at all costs. Learning and making an effort are both encouraged when one has a growth mentality. If you have faith that you can become better at anything, you will be more driven to study and put in the effort necessary to do so. The input provided through criticism is appreciated and fully taken into account. The commitment to keeping at something, even when it's difficult or when things aren't going as planned, is one of the defining characteristics of a development mindset.

This strategy is in line with the growth mentality, yet many managers behave toward their employees as though they are incapable of developing themselves. This kind of thinking is the root cause of many of the actions that workers who are leaving a company discuss in their departure interviews.

Quite some time ago, I was requested to guide an attorney through the steps necessary to become an equity partner in a famous international law firm. The business in question was located in another country. I was given a rundown by Human Resources. It is said that he is a very good lawyer. However, he refers to his collaborators as "units of production," and he lacks the patience to cultivate such relationships.

Take a look at Figure 5 -- Mindsets for People Management -- to determine which mindset best reflects the approach used by this lawyer.

Figure 5: Different Mental Approaches to Managing People

Unfortunately, since he saw his coworkers as mere units of production, he would blame them for poor performance and refuse to invest any time in their professional growth or in contemplating the ways in which he was responsible for their failures via the expectations he had set for them. A mentality like this might either persuade individuals to quit the company or have a harmful effect on the self-esteem and confidence of those who continue to work there.

A boss who takes on the role of savior is just as unproductive as their employees.

The Rescuers have an excessive amount of responsibility, and in an effort to be pleasant, they impede the progress of their people, which results in frustration for those individuals. Rescue workers are unable to expand their teams, and as a result, they generally overwork themselves and reach a career plateau.

A growth mentality is the proper one to adopt for yourself, and one that you should foster in the minds of your employees. This frame of mind results from having faith in your team's ability to learn, develop, become better, and achieve success despite the difficulties or setbacks that lie ahead.

Consideration: Which of the following describes your default position: blamer, rescuer, growth, or any mix of the three.

Why does having a growth mindset make a difference?

The Rosenthal effect, also known as the Pygmalion effect, is the name given to the findings of a research that demonstrated that when instructors anticipated improved performance from their students, those students actually delivered improved results. The findings of the research provided evidence in favor of the premise that the expectations of others might either positively or adversely impact the experience of reality. Therefore, if you anticipate excellence from your team, it will result in increased performance from them.

Increasing Your Capabilities As A Leader

In this chapter, we are going to discuss various exercises that you may perform in order to strengthen yourself on each of the characteristics that were discussed in the previous chapter. You are going to uncover real world exercises and questions that you may ask yourself throughout this chapter in order to enhance your leadership abilities and become a stronger leader. These activities and questions are designed to help you become a better leader.

How to Strengthen Your Own Integrity: Nobody wants to believe that they are dishonest, yet there are a lot of different reasons why you can decide to exaggerate something or leave out a portion of the truth. The following are some of these reasons:

Making a positive impression on others; protecting oneself from the humiliation of having committed an error; evading a penalty for having engaged in inappropriate behavior.

When serving these aims, it is often convenient to obscure or omit facts. You may, however, help yourself become a more honest person by doing the things that I am about to list below.

When you tell lies, you should think about who you are trying to persuade. One way to encourage oneself to be more honest is to consider the people who will be impacted by one's actions.

Consider the kind of person you want to become rather than concentrating on the things you would rather not do. If you are subject to certain regulations, you will most likely violate those regulations whenever there is a low probability that you will be detected. People who are honest always act morally responsible, even when no one is watching.

Being honest is much more than just avoiding untruths. It is also important to not take longer breaks than necessary, to tell the whole truth, and to stand up for other people when you see that they are being treated unjustly. Admit to the wrongdoings that you have committed; if you aren't willing to take responsibility for your actions, you aren't being honest.

If you find yourself in a position where you have to lie to get out of it, say the truth to yourself. Recognize that your response was inadequate to the challenge at hand and make a commitment to improve in the future. If you claim you are going to try harder the next time, don't simply say it and shrug it off; show that you mean it by improving your performance.

Take into consideration the questions that follow:

Who exactly are you hurting when you lie and cheat? Consider not just yourself and the other people who will be immediately impacted by the situation, but also the other people who will be indirectly impacted by it. Take, for instance, the scenario in which you and the other members of your team are working on a project that requires you to remain late in order to finish it. You explain to your colleagues that you are going to work on something on your computer, but instead you opt to spend the next half an hour scrolling through your various social media accounts. Your decision will have immediate repercussions on your team. Along with your own family, the families of the other members of your team are going to be impacted as well. When your exhausted staff gets behind the wheel and drives home longer than was required, you are also directly affecting every other person that is on the road.

What kind of person do you want to be? What do you hope people will remember you for? When others have the impression that you are exaggerating or ignoring the facts, their level of confidence in you will gradually decrease. Do you want for others to put their faith in you?

Think back to a moment when someone lied to you or misled you in some way. How did you experience it? What was your response to that?

Consider the instances in which you have lied or been dishonest. After it was over, were you truthful with yourself? Or did you disregard it as something inconsequential and go on?

Do you live up to your promises? Do you keep things to yourself? Are you dependable?

How to Develop Your Capacity for Empathy: There are a lot of individuals who may make progress in their jobs, but then all of a sudden they hit a wall because of their lack of people skills. Leaders who lack the ability to interact effectively with others often discover that they are unable to assemble a group of individuals who are eager to perform quality work for them, as well as a group that is unsuccessful at working together to complete a task. The following are characteristics of persons who are not good with other people:

acting in a manner that is insensitive when asking a coworker for anything; giving the impression that they never listen when others are speaking; showing intolerance for other ways of doing tasks.

There are a lot of steps you can take to improve your ability to empathize with other people and, as a result, become more of a people person.

Consider the situation from the perspective of the other person. When you are able to accomplish this, you will have a better chance of seeing that other people are not mean-spirited, irrational, or obstinate; rather, they are just responding to a situation based on the knowledge they have. If you are able to understand things from the perspective of another person, you will be in a better position to communicate with that person and will have a greater chance of arriving at a solution that will be acceptable to all parties involved.

It is not enough to just view things from another person's perspective; you also need to admit that you see it from their perspective. When you acknowledge another person's viewpoint, it does not imply that you share that viewpoint; rather, it demonstrates that you are open to the possibility that other individuals may have viewpoints that are dissimilar to your own.

Consider the stance you're taking. If you go into a situation with an open mind and a positive attitude, you give yourself opportunity to be more empathic to the other individuals you are working with, which is a huge benefit to everyone involved.

Being empathic requires a significant amount of active listening on your behalf. It is vital to pay attention to the whole of the information that is being sent to you, and this requires you to listen with more than just your ears. It is essential to listen with both of your ears in order to not only hear the words that are being spoken but also the tone in which they are being uttered. Additionally, it is essential to "listen with your eyes" and pay attention to the body language of the person you are conversing with. Pay attention to your gut feelings; they will let you know whether the other person is hiding anything from you. Listen from your heart, and consider what you believe the other person is experiencing.

If you are unclear about anything, you should ask the other person to clarify their stance. If you ask the individual to explain why they have the view, they are more likely to do so when you are empathic since it is much simpler for them to do so. To get a discussion off on the right foot and make sure that everyone is on the same page, you may use this easy and clear technique. Do not be hesitant to inquire about the other person's needs and desires.

Take into consideration the questions that follow:

Do you have a habit of paying attention to the persons you are talking to, or do you often find yourself thinking about something else?

Are you paying close attention to what is being said and picking up on the important phrases and words that are being uttered?

Do you tend to make a reply that is only partially thought through, which demonstrates that you weren't listening, or do you answer in a way that is encouraging?

When you start a new discussion, do you go in with a preconceived notion of how it's going to turn out, or do you keep an open mind?

A Guide to Developing Your Optimism: The natural perspective of many individuals is one of the situation being worse than it really is. This is something that comes naturally to certain individuals from the time they are young. If you want to demonstrate excellent leadership qualities, you must train your mind to think in a more optimistic manner, even if it comes more naturally to you to think in a pessimistic way. There are a lot of actions you can do at work that can help you become a more upbeat and positive person.

Take into consideration what is succeeding in each given circumstance. Think on the things that are going well rather than focusing solely on the things that aren't working out the way you want them to. If you're having trouble getting along with one of the members on your team, try shifting your viewpoint rather than concentrating on the aspects of that person that you find challenging. It's possible that a member of your team consistently gets their job done early, arrives on time for work, or is excellent at inspiring the other members of the team.

Adapt your strategy for playing the "What If" game. The "What If" game is played in a pessimistic manner by many individuals. For example, one can say, "If I get fired, I won't be able to pay my bills, and I'll get kicked out of my apartment..." Put a more upbeat spin on the situation by telling yourself, "Even if I do get fired, I have a solid skill set, and I have gained a lot of experience working here." I have established some contacts, and I am certain that I will be able to find another role in which I can be of assistance. In the meanwhile, I'm going to concentrate on making sure that I'm not replaceable and making sure that my task is completed on time every time.

Recognize that you, along with everyone else, are liable to make errors. Do not criticize or assign blame to a fellow member of the team if they make a mistake or are unsuccessful at anything. Instead, you should concentrate on figuring out how you can contribute to their success. They will respect your assistance and see you as a wonderful leader because you are demonstrating to them that you appreciate the efforts they are making to improve, and they will realize that you are someone to whom they can turn for support. This goes to not just concentrating on the errors your team members may make along the route, but also recognizing when they are doing something exceptional and giving them credit for it.

Activities For The Development Of Leadership

You will get an understanding of how to acquire the abilities necessary to become a leader by reading this chapter. You will discover how to improve your ability to communicate effectively as well as your ability to solve problems. You will also learn how to evaluate the work and performance of other people in a fair and honest manner, in addition to analyzing your own work and performance. You will also learn how to browse various projects and how to multitask so that you may grow in a number of different areas at the same time. The ability to make intelligent and efficient use of one's time is an absolute need for everyone in a leadership position. Skills in time management allow this. This chapter will teach you how to improve your time management abilities so that you may concentrate on the things that will provide you with the greatest benefits. This chapter will also show you how to locate and keep your motivation and inspiration going, which is not the least important thing it will teach you. Working on developing your own capabilities is going to be a tough endeavor, and sustaining consistency is going to need understanding of the wants and desires that lay underlying your goals. As a result of this, the next chapter will also concentrate on things that you can do to train your motivation and keep both your drive and your inspiration going strong.

The Importance of Developing What Are Called "Soft Skills"

Working hard and picking up new abilities won't be enough to get you forward in your professional field; you'll need to do more than that. Building a successful career requires the acquisition of "soft skills," in addition to "technical skills." These so-called "soft skills" are difficult to quantify, and they do not have a direct bearing on your level of performance. Instead, they provide you the opportunity to gradually advance in your profession by giving you practice in the skills necessary to become a leader. In spite of what you may have believed, there is no such thing as a leader who is born with innate authority. Everyone has the potential to become a leader if they put in the necessary amount of work and practice. Even if some individuals have a greater natural potential for this than others, there is always something that you can do to develop your own leadership abilities and become someone who other people will want to follow.

Maintaining a level of self-control. Every effective leader must possess the quality of discipline as one of their defining traits. You may more effectively lead by example if you have more discipline in both your personal and professional lives. Because of this, everyone around you will be inspired to exercise more self-control. In general, others who follow in your footsteps will evaluate your capabilities based on how ethically and methodically you carry out your duties. To put this into practice, all that is required is to ensure that all of your obligations, including deadlines and appointments, are met.

Project Management That Includes Navigating and Multitasking

When you are trying to advance in your job, the biggest obstacle you will face is being unorganized. Participation in several ongoing projects will be required if you want to advance in your career, whether it be via the expansion of your existing company or the acquisition of higher-level roles. To be successful in working in a number of different areas at the same time, you will need to have excellent organizational abilities and a strong dedication to self-discipline. After all, if you don't know how to plan, set priorities, and take care of yourself so that you can stay focused, enthusiastic, and inspired while juggling many endeavors, it's very easy for things to slip through the cracks. In the perspective of other people, demonstrating that you are trustworthy and reliable by adhering to healthy routines such as getting enough rest by going to bed on time and rising early so that you can get a head start on your workday is something that will help you go forward in your life and career. This sort of a disciplined and balanced lifestyle will deliver ideal levels of energy, a wealth of creative ideas, and a keen and analytical mind to distribute these resources across a variety of high-impact jobs.

To establish oneself as a capable leader, it will be required for you to participate in a variety of tasks. You should constantly set an example for others to follow when you are trying to become a leader. You have an obligation to participate in all of the initiatives that are currently being carried out in your industry. Because being a leader implies becoming someone who other people will want to follow, having a strong presence and maintaining a razor's edge concentration are both needed. To have the desire to follow someone, one must have faith in that person's judgment and believe that they are benefiting in some way from the leader's efforts. You depend on the notion that others have that following in your footsteps will help them progress their own professions. To do this, you will need to continue to serve as a model for the person(s) they want to be. In order to accomplish this, you will need to demonstrate that you are an important asset by accepting responsibility. Managing many tasks at once and being able to switch gears between them are both skills that may be learned with some time and effort. The following are the important measures for managing projects while simultaneously juggling many tasks:

Determine the outcomes.

Every undertaking need to have a purpose that contributes to a larger vision, whether that vision pertains to your professional or private life.identifying a goal for the project is not a particularly challenging task; nevertheless, identifying the outcomes you need to display is the critical phase that many people skip. Define what each project will bring into your life and company by outlining everything you anticipate seeing, such as deadlines, quantities, percentages, items, and so on. In addition, each project has to have its own set of to-do lists, which should include the many stages, actions, and responsibilities of everyone involved.

Make assignments.

Every undertaking calls for a committed group of individuals, and you need to give primary attention to recruiting those who possess the highest levels of skill and experience so that they can assist you in achieving your goals. At work, responsibilities need to be allocated in accordance with one's credentials and years of experience, all the while ensuring that choices are not influenced by favoritism or political considerations of any kind.

Prepare a thorough plan.

It is not advisable to micromanage your team since doing so will discourage them. Instead, you should prepare each and every stage and step of the process while also ensuring that every member is aware of their specific function. Indicators of success, performance, and outcomes, as well as dangers, should be clearly established for the purposes of monitoring the effectiveness of the project.

Prepare yourself to multitask.

When all of your projects have been meticulously planned, you should examine your responsibilities to determine which of the activities may be completed in parallel, and which of the responsibilities need your total attention.

Set aside certain amounts of time and resources.

After determining which particular activities can be completed simultaneously and which must be completed one at a time, the next step is to assess and plan the amount of time and resources that will be required to complete the tasks. It is essential that your assessments be grounded on reality and not just wishful thinking. In addition, while developing a schedule, it is important to provide for at least 10–20 percent additional time and investment in case unanticipated challenges arise.

Make a schedule for yourself.

If you keep yourself informed of the chores that are still outstanding, multitasking shouldn't be too tough for you. Because of this, it is essential to block off sufficient amounts of time in your agenda in order to accommodate the activities that are required. If you are having trouble with this, you always have the option of employing a consultant to assist you with effective time management.

Taking on more duties requires you to push yourself outside of your comfort zone and widen the range of your skillset in order to meet the demands of the new role. To perform well across a variety of tasks and responsibilities will demand a commitment of both time and effort. You will be able to acquire more initiative if you learn how to take on and manage bigger duties and then put what you've learned into practice. Evaluate whether or not you'll need to master new abilities in order to complete the assignments before taking on many projects at once. In the event that it is necessary, you should enroll in various classes, seminars, and courses that will provide you with the appropriate information for the new company endeavor.

Communication with Participation

Learning how to communicate effectively is necessary for one's personal progress. The act of acquiring new knowledge also contributes, at least to some extent, to the development of one's communication abilities. The exchange of appropriate messages and information is often the central organizing principle of communication within classrooms and other educational settings. Participating in this process enables you to improve your ability to converse and interact with others, as well as learn how to communicate in an appropriate manner. In addition to this, there is a common correlation between education and overall health and well-being. On the other hand, being an entrepreneur and being in a leadership role both need a significant amount of effort to be put into developing one's communication abilities. In order to be a good leader, you will need to put in a lot of hard effort to improve the communication within your own team. Enhancing your own and your team's communication abilities may be accomplished with little effort by participating in role play exercises. Learning how to ask questions with open-ended answers is the objective of the practice. It is crucial to learn how to ask open-ended questions in order to have effective communication, since doing so provides every person with the chance to contribute their perspective on the subject being discussed. The following is the exercise's proper form:

First, one person should leave the room while the other participants are intending to ask them open-ended questions on a certain subject, with the necessity to include inquiries such as: Who? What? Why? Where? How? and other similar questions. This should continue until the person who left the room returns. You should go for inquiries that are light and revolve on a volunteer's personal or professional life as much as possible. The team will begin asking open-ended questions as soon as the individual enters the room, and they will continue to do so until the person has provided a complete response to the issue. By practicing active listening and taking mental notes on pertinent information, you and the other members of your team will improve your ability to communicate with one another. This activity is one of a wide variety of communication-enhancing activities and exercises available; nevertheless, it is unique in that it improves both listening and speaking abilities. It teaches you and the other members of the team how to ask questions in a confident and courteous manner, all while maintaining your concentration on the information you are trying to get.

Unbiased Focus on the Situation

One of the most crucial aspects of being a successful leader is developing the ability to follow the lead of others. When you pay attention to reasoning and accept the criticism and viewpoints of others, even those with which you disagree, it demonstrates that you are an objective person who does not criticize others based on the degree to which they agree with what you say. This demonstrates that you are an impartial person who listens to and evaluates the opinions of other people. This demonstrates a reasonable, non-judgmental, and non-prejudiced character, which is reliable and trustworthy, and it is a quality worth having.

Awareness of the Current Situation

Having situational awareness, also known as awareness of the current circumstance, enables one to perceive the wider picture and helps to avoid issues from arising. This is a crucial talent that can assist you in managing time-sensitive tasks and seizing possibilities that you would not have seen in any other circumstance.

Participation in Full Swing

The ability to communicate effectively requires not just active engagement but also an assertive attitude that is courteous and free of hostility in terms of tone of voice, facial expression, and overall body language. You will find it easier to cultivate connections that are solid and based on mutual respect if you engage in active conversation. In addition to that, you will get the opportunity to hone your public speaking skills in order to appropriately disseminate your message. under addition, developing the ability to communicate effectively under trying circumstances is an important component of developing the abilities to convince and influence others. To influence the opinions of others, one must engage in constructive conversation and possess a high level of emotional intelligence in order to comprehend the driving forces behind the behaviors of others. People will follow you if they believe that they will profit in some way from what you are doing. You need to be aware of the aims and intentions of other people and use your own abilities of emotional intelligence to your own maximum advantage. In addition, you need to be aware of the objectives and intentions of other people.

She then went on to say, "We can comprehend more in details:

Cultural Diversity: In this day and age of technological advancement and increased globalization, a great number of businesses are striving to achieve success in the area of cultural diversity in the workplace. more employee engagement may result from more cultural variety. If a corporation actively promotes cultural tolerance and acceptance in the workplace, it will instantly be able to choose from a more diverse pool of applicants for available positions.

Age diversity refers to the fact that different age groups may be represented within an organization. Each generation, from the older, more experienced staff members to the middle-aged staff members to the millennials to the new college graduates or even the teenagers, has its own set of distinctive characteristics. There is no question that various age groups need for different approaches to management. It is the duty of a leader to ensure that different generations are represented in the workforce in an effective manner.

Social Diversity: It is the responsibility of a leader to ensure that the social status of a group member does not cause discord among the members of the group. It is important that the member not have feelings of isolation or insecurity.

Diversity of Disabilities: The challenges that disabled individuals experience in the job are quite similar to those that women confront. There are, without a doubt, a number of occupations that people with disabilities are unable to do; yet, there are millions of other vocations that they are nonetheless able to accomplish. When it comes to impaired workers, it is the job of a leader to make sure that the positions they are given are appropriate for their skill level. The frame of mind to adopt in this situation is to concentrate on what they are able to do and do within the bounds of their skill and the restrictions imposed by their impairment.

Gender Diversity: Traditionally, various sorts of labor have been segregated based on a person's gender. People had the misconception that only women could work in nursing, and that males predominated in some engineering disciplines. It made a veiled reference to the differences in the capacities, both physical and emotional, that exist between the sexes.

Today, I'm pleased to see people of both sexes working in every industry. Companies have a greater duty in this area to preserve harmonious relationships among its staff members, regardless of whether those staff members are men, women, or LGBTQ. Ensure that no one looks down or up on a certain gender. Instead of focusing on gender, a leader should foster a diverse team in order to make the most of everyone's talents and abilities.

Diversification at the National Level: To have staff of different nationalities assigned in different nations is one of the most important tactics used by all

500 corporations on the Fortune 500 list.

A leader may make use of their talents, such as knowing the cultural norms and value structures of the nation they are leading. It makes it easier to engage with clients, get better agreements, and gain an advantage over other businesses in the industry.

The key to a prosperous future for any company is to cultivate an inclusive culture across the company. Along with a workforce that is comprised of people from a variety of cultural backgrounds, the client base of today is also diverse ethnically. In the lack of a culture of diversity and inclusion, an organization is seen as being unwelcoming and inflexible to its members' needs. The only duty of those in positions of leadership is to foster an environment in which everyone feels welcome.

"I really appreciate the thoughtfulness! As a leader, there are a lot of things to think about when it comes to diversity, but for an average person, it's simply a term. Do we approach millennials in a different manner because we believe they will become an important component of the age diversity in the workforce? If so, then how?"

She responded by saying, "According to the statistics, in the next five years, 75% of the global workforce will be composed of millennials. This means that this group will occupy the majority of leadership roles over the course of the coming decade." They will be responsible for making crucial choices that have a significant impact on the cultures of workplaces and the lives of individuals. Their one-of-a-kind viewpoint on diversity is the result of a concoction of a wide range of experiences, varied backgrounds, and distinct points of view.

Millennials nowadays have a greater awareness and sensitivity for the environment in which they work. They not only aim to produce work of a high quality, but they also want their work to have an impact on the community in which they reside. According to the surveys, more than sixty percent of people looking for work consider diversity to be an important consideration in evaluating firms and career opportunities. Another survey showed that more than 80 percent of millennials are actively engaged in their job when their company has a diverse workplace culture.

Since I was under the impression that this was the case, I posed the question, "What are the benefits of diversity in organization?"

Aaron said, "Many, I would think diversity brings in some amazing benefits, although looking back on it, I'm sure it has its challenges." The following is a good way to describe it."

Chancellor Angela Merkel is the most powerful woman in the world for these ten reasons.

Since she took office in 2005, Angela Merkel has fundamentally altered the political landscape in Germany. As a result of her accomplishments both at home and abroad, she has been named to the most powerful women list by Forbes eight times. The following are the top ten reasons why many people consider Angela Merkel to be the most powerful woman in the world.

Her tenacity while serving in government

The current chancellor of Germany, Angela Merkel, is now serving her fourth term in office. She has remained in office for this long not just because she is at the pinnacle of her authority, but also because Konrad Adenauer is the only chancellor who has remained in office for such a long period as she has. Helmut Kohl and Helmut Schmidt were in office for somewhat longer periods of time, but none of them were able to outlast Merkel. She will be remembered in the annals of German and European history as the ruler who maintained her power for a considerable number of years and who also amassed a number of significant victories during her time in office.

Europe and the same currency

Because of her success in resolving the issue surrounding the euro, she is now considered to be the de facto leader of Europe. This recognition is due to the fact that she was able to resolve the crisis. Merkel is still in control of the purse strings as far as Athens is concerned, and that fact will be much more sharply felt if the left-wing party, with its vows to forsake debt and defy the austerity measures, wins the election. Merkel has issued a stern warning to the effect that the eurozone may continue to exist even without Greece's participation. Her determination on imposing austerity measures and reforms on the rest of Europe in the pattern of Germany, rather than giving in to the persistent calls to flood the markets with even more money, resulted in her winning very few friends. Her unwavering commitment to assisting those in need earned her the acclaim of many, and it was largely because to this that she was able to win the support of all of Germany's residents. Because of the situation, she was forced to demonstrate to the public her talents as a genuine leader. On the other hand, she wouldn't have been able to demonstrate her ability in managing problems if there hadn't been a crisis. Her proclamation, in which she argues that if the euro collapses, Europe would undoubtedly fall as well, served as the source of her drive. Due to the fact that it is yet too soon to render a judgment on her policies, this proclamation also highlights the historical opportunity that she confronts. First and foremost, she has to save the euro, which is still in a precarious position. During her eight years in office as chancellor, she was successful in bringing the European effort of rescuing the euro to a successful conclusion.

The economy overall

throughout the time of the financial crisis in Europe, the majority of the European leaders were taken out of power by the financial crisis; nevertheless, Merkel has flourished throughout this time owing to her unrelenting efforts in lessening the severity of the crisis. Merkel has completely averted a protracted recession that was about to take place in Germany at the period of the global economic crisis. She has been effective in developing and designing an economic system in which people put in less hours, but their wages are supplemented by the government rather than the companies for which they work. Due to the fact that they were able to take advantage of certain advantageous circumstances throughout the crisis, such as cheap interest on bonds, Germany was able to grow despite the global economic crisis. A shortage of qualified employees, for which Germany will require immigrants, will be one of Merkel's future issues. She will also have to cope with the public infrastructure that is not supported, an education system that is not standard, and a lack of qualified workers. The cumulative impact of all of these factors will be catastrophic for the economy.

Energy policy revisions

Shortly after the catastrophe that occurred at Fukushima, Angela Merkel issued a statement stating that eight of Germany's 17 nuclear reactors would be shut down, and the remaining reactors would be phased out by the year 2022. The exit was necessary as a phase of a long-term shift to alternative energy sources known as the "Energiewende." This transition was the cause for the exit. This specific measure garnered substantial support for Merkel across the political spectrum, and it improved Germany's reputation as a world-leader in the reform of energy policy in an attempt to combat global warming.

Her about-face was seen to be a normal attitude given the situation. Merkel has always maintained her stance that the nuclear reactors should be allowed to remain operational. Some individuals believe that she took advantage of the emotionally charged situation caused by the Fukushima disaster.

Eliminating mandatory military service

Merkel was able to provide her support to the objective of Defense Minister Karl-Theodor zu Guttenberg, who endeavored to do all in his power to do away with mandatory military service for men. They had to contend with a wide range of misconceptions on the part of many conservative lawmakers. As part of efforts to lower the size of the military from about 240,000 troops to a professional and considerably fitter army of 170,000 personnel, the armed services decided in July 2011 to do away with mandatory military service, marking the end of the military's first half-century of existence. As a result of Ursula von der Leyen's tenure as Merkel's defense minister, the Bundeswehr now provides a child-care service and allows employees more leeway in their scheduling. Both of these aspects demonstrated Merkel's dedication to the institution of the family.

The German term for child support is known as Elterngeld.

The German government under Merkel's leadership initiated the "Elterngeld" or parent benefit program in 2007 as a means of lending financial assistance to families with children. It is comparable to maternity pay, except it may be received by either parent. The program's objectives are to reduce the monetary strain that is placed on families and to increase the very low birthrate in Germany. The program is sponsored by taxes and enables parents to take turns taking up to 14 months off work following the birth of a child, during which time they may receive up to 67% of their regular pay. Merkel battled vehemently against the opponents of Elterngeld within her own conservative coalition. Having proclaimed it to be one of the cornerstones of her government policy, Merkel defended the right for fathers to take time off to raise their children in particular. The program did not have the intended effect of increasing the birthrate, but it did have a significant effect on family life in Germany, notably on the lives of working moms.

The bare minimum pay

It is still believed to be to Merkel's credit that a minimum wage was implemented under her watch, after years of lobbying in an attempt to ameliorate social inequality. This is despite the fact that it was led by her coalition partners, the Social Democrats, but it is still considered to be to Merkel's credit that it was introduced. The rate of €8.50 (or £7) per hour was implemented on January 1, 2015, and its proponents claim that it would help combat rising social divides and address increasing income disparity. It is also intended to increase the earnings of those individuals who have, in effect, been subjected to a pay freeze since businesses in Germany felt that low wages were vital for the country's firms to preserve their competitive advantage.

Russia in international politics

Merkel's efforts in the realm of international policy have been successful; most recently, she has made sure that she maintains an open line of communication with Vladimir Putin, the president of Russia, regarding the conflict in Crimea. Because of her upbringing in East Germany, she is very familiar with Russian culture and speaks Russian to an excellent standard. Despite the fact that she does not like Putin, the person who always lets his Labrador run loose around her despite being aware of her fear of dogs, she feels that it is her responsibility to keep communicating with him. Thanks to her upbringing in East Germany, she is able to speak Russian to an excellent standard. She has highlighted to other western leaders that putting too much pressure on him may force Russia into political and economic disarray, which would not be good for Russia, nor would it be good for Germany, nor would it be good for Europe.

thriving in a male-dominated environment as a woman who attends a party

Not only has Merkel's election as leader of the Christian Democratic Union, which is a mostly Catholic party with its origins in West Germany and is controlled by men, but she is also a Protestant and an East German woman who does not have children. Her election has transformed not just the party, but maybe even German society. She is Germany's first female political leader and is renowned for having passed a large number of males on her route to the top. According to the European council on foreign relations, Merkel was a significant contributor to the transformation of the thoroughly conservative party into "one of the pillars of the new German consensus." This has resulted in a new policy direction on everything from energy reform to family and women's rights, including the recent decision to implement female quotas into the boardroom. This has also resulted in a new policy orientation on everything from energy reform to family and women's rights.

Management Of Both Leadership And Time Is Essential.

To be a leader, one has to cultivate abilities in time management that are appropriate for someone in that role. Life is characterized by the unchanging reality that the adage "time waits for no one" is true. Nobody can stop time, and it doesn't care who you are. Regardless matter who you are, where you've been, or what you've evolved into, he will not wait. He will not hold his breath. When time is squandered, it is impossible to get it back, and once it has been lost, it can never be recovered. It does not matter what may have occurred to you or how essential the additional time may be; time will not slow down for you. Therefore, in order to prevent having regrets, it is necessary to efficiently manage the limited amount of time we have. Visionary leaders are the only ones who can make effective time management apparent. Without vision, there is no good cause to efficiently manage one's time. In order for a leader to have efficient time management, he has to handle the larger visions first, before moving on to the more specific concepts. The common misconception held by leaders is that they never have sufficient free time, which is incorrect for a number of reasons. The use of technology has transformed the use of time into a tool that is far more productive than it first seems to be. Nobody is born knowing how to efficiently manage their time; rather, this is a talent that must be acquired throughout one's life. Therefore, it is possible for everyone to do. Keeping track of the time you spend doing things is the most effective strategy to increase your productivity. You may increase your productivity in other ways as well, for as by finding a solution to your difficulty with time management and devoting more of your time to the accomplishment of your objectives.

When you get better at making efficient use of time, you will notice that your life starts to function with fewer hiccups and more consistency. It is a grave error on our part to believe that we can reduce our time commitments. It is impossible to create more time; rather, each day passes at a predetermined pace. Nobody can completely master the art of time management; all we can do is learn to manage ourselves and the things we do with the time we have. A leader who focuses more on the desired outcome rather than on what has to be done will often discover that higher outcomes are really happening under their watch. When it comes to some areas of leadership, the course that we follow is of far more significance than the rate at which we are working to realize our ideas. In the realm of effective time management, the ability to precisely identify a goal and then pursue that objective in the appropriate order of importance is one of the most important abilities that one may possess. An appraisal of how essential one aim is in comparison to another is used to determine the order of priority.

Making a list in which certain items are ranked higher than others in terms of their importance is what we mean when we talk about setting priorities for the work that we undertake. It will be much simpler for you to successfully manage your time after this list has been arranged according to the relevance and urgency of each item on it. Technology has made it much simpler to plan, and a wide variety of mobile applications can now keep track of what has to be done on your behalf. Nowadays, the cell phone is the item that is always the nearest to us, which makes it an appropriate planner since it can be used at any moment. As we take on more of life's responsibilities and positions of leadership, the challenge of maximizing the use of our time becomes more significant.

The following are some examples of several things that a leader may do to properly manage their time:

Gaining control over the decision-making process rather than the choices themselves is the focus of this skill set.

Keeping your attention only on doing one task at a time.

Create the mentality necessary to be successful with your time.

by being constantly aware of your field of view.

Goal setting on a daily, weekly, monthly, and yearly basis should be planned.

by determining what they are and making connections between them.

Getting rid of the pointless and useless stuff by throwing them away.

by setting personal targets for each objective and committing to meeting those deadlines.

by respecting the time of others and avoiding doing things that take up unnecessary amounts of your own time.

ensuring that one's calendars are correct and being consistent with them.

Recognizing when an activity, policy, or method has reached its completion.

via the practice of delegating anything that can be.

Putting aside some time for introspection.

Utilizing checklists and lists of things to do.

by rearranging priorities in light of newly assigned responsibilities.

Is It True That Women Have Greater Emotional Intelligence Than Men?

As you may have observed (given that it has been many a sub-point throughout this book, so far), this term comes up very often while addressing emotional intelligence. A great number of individuals believe that having such compassion is the most important factor in thoroughly comprehending any topic. Your capacity to comprehend and manage your emotions has a significant impact on the quality of your relationships with other people.

In terms of the scientific study of empathy, this process takes place in a particular region of our brains, which is responsible for gathering information from the rest of our bodies. When we experience empathy for another person, it is essentially our mind attempting to mimic the feelings that are being felt by that other person. A certain region of our brain makes use of our complete physiology in order to detect what the other person is feeling and to assist in providing information to our own thoughts about it.

It just so happens that the knowledge that is gained via the act of empathy is stored in the minds of women for a far longer period of time than it is in the minds of men. They have a greater capacity to draw on their feelings in order to justify the behavior of another person. The ability to empathize with other people and share in their joys and sorrows comes far more naturally to women than it does to men.

It's far less probable that such emotions will be stored in a man's brain. They are able to turn the switch off and start using a new section of their brain. Because of this, the individual's mind is unable to build a recollection or conduct an analysis of the emotional state that the other person is now experiencing. Because of the way their biological systems work, men are less prone to have their decisions influenced by their emotions.

Discussions and negotiations

Naturally, we have a lot of tools at our disposal thanks to our improved emotional intelligence that may assist us in being successful in negotiations. The first skill we need to work on is developing a heightened sense of self-awareness and learning to name the feelings that we are experiencing. When we are placed in stressful circumstances, it is quite probable that we may experience a range of different intense emotions. To sustain our leverage, though, it will be to our advantage to rein in those urges and keep them under control at all times. Because of this, a more stringent degree of control is going to be necessary.

In general, it is important for you to communicate your thoughts in a healthy manner; yet, in this circumstance, you do not want to reveal your sentiments since you do not want them to be misinterpreted. To maintain composure and keep one's emotions under control, it might be helpful to consciously name the feelings one is experiencing. You may reduce a significant amount of the effect it has on you just by knowing that it exists.

After you have accomplished that, you may engage in acts of empathy to improve your understanding of how to negotiate with the other party. You don't have to accept their offer at face value; rather than doing that, you may try to interpret the meaning behind what they are saying in order to establish new footholds. You will have a better chance of comprehending the feelings that the other person is experiencing if you are more open to the verbal and nonverbal expressions of communication that they are making available to you. Make use of reason to derive the circumstances that led them to take the viewpoint that they do so that you may provide persuasive arguments in your favor.

You will simply utilize your social skills to come across as a respectable and likeable professional. This is maybe the most crucial thing that you will do. It is impossible to overstate the value of acquiring the skills necessary to become an effective communicator. These conferences are a two-way interaction, and if you go into them with a positive attitude, you will find that you have a lot better time. In point of fact, you should make an effort to quit thinking about negotiations as a win-or-lose scenario. In truth, talks are a win-win situation for both sides. Everyone will be in a better mood after the conversation if you are able to successfully reframe the topic in this manner and utilize your emotional intelligence to communicate this to the other side.

Who Are Some of the Most Effective Leaders?

It goes without saying that a person's gender has no bearing on whether or not they will be an effective leader. Everyone has something to gain by interacting with people of the opposing gender. Everyone has the potential to acquire the abilities necessary to be a credible authority figure; nevertheless, it's possible that various challenges stand in the way of each person reaching their full emotional intelligence potential.

Women have an advantage over males when it comes to demonstrating their emotional intelligence since it is generally accepted that women are more in tune with their emotions and, as a result, have more experience demonstrating emotional intelligence than men do. In the United States, on average, women and girls begin their formal education in social matters at a younger age than men and boys do. This statement may or may not be accurate. Men, on the other hand, may have had the perception that they were not meant to develop their emotional intelligence and, as a result, were under the impression that they needed to discover this trait on their own or overcome some kind of training that discouraged them from studying their emotions.

It is too broad of a generalization to say that one specific skill will make either men or women better leaders. However, it has been demonstrated that the initiative and openness required to learn and improve one's emotional intelligence is the same kind of initiative and openness that is required to become more competent in positions of authority. This ability also takes into account logical reasoning and rational thought. Each individual, whether male or female, brings a unique set of skills and experiences to the table while serving in a managerial capacity.

Anyone who is willing to cooperate with others and work on improving themselves (both of which are necessary components in developing emotional intelligence) is someone who has the desire and courage to pursue management roles. This may mean overcoming difficulties that are placed in your path while moving up the professional ladder, or it may mean overcoming societal barriers that inhibited your emotional development prior to being an adult and requiring you to overcome these obstacles before becoming an adult. If you are able to manage the relationships to prosper despite these problems, then you have been putting your high EQ to work for you and shown that you are excellent material for leadership. If you are able to do this, then you have shown that you are good leadership material.

It Is Essential To Be Competent. Certainty Is Of The Utmost Importance.

FROM THE STORY OF THE MOUSETRAP:

When the mouse noticed the mousetrap, what was the first thing that he did? He did not move. What are some of the things that he might have done differently?

IN ALL ACTUALITY:

In the event that you sound the alarm in the middle of an emergency, nobody will want to be near to you since you are the leader.In point of fact, everyone need to keep their distance from you!

A state of emergency is not the time to lose your composure and panic. Now is the moment to maintain your composure! When you converse while in a state of stress, you end up conveying your panic to the other person.

The irony of competence:

A great number of people who are competent in terms of their talents, gifts, and experience get stuck in their lives because they need assurance. Remember that having the capacity is important, but having the confidence to use it is critical. Whenever two people work along amicably, the one who has the greater amount of conspicuous assurance has the benefit. It should come as no surprise that the word "advantage" originates from the archaic sport of arm wrestling. The one who comes out on top gets his hand placed on top of the hand of the loser. He is in a better position. Simply said, if you want to come out on top in your administration sport, you need to have a higher level of confidence.

SEVEN CHARACTERISTICS That Improve Along with Increasing Confidence:

1. Having courage

2. an attitude of mental composure

3. The ability to think clearly

4. Independence from external direction

5. Capacity to Overcome Obstacles and Challenges

6. a certain mind-set

7. Quickness of response

If you go back through history, you'll find that the great majority of the outstanding pioneers whose contributions we value now didn't start out with all of the essential capabilities. Despite this, they participated in a variety of causes because they thought it was necessary. They felt more confident in their decisions the further they got engaged. The more confident they were, the more adept they became at what they were doing. The wait patiently for excellent talent might be an ageless ability; begin with the conviction that you will get the ability eventually.

CONFIDENCE In Contrast With ARrogance

People often inquire as to the differences between absolute confidence and pompous behavior. The characteristics of unjustified childishness and disinterest for the viewpoints and significance of other people are characteristics of arrogance. The guiding principle is as follows: arrogance is defined as the belief that one is capable of doing anything. The belief that I am capable of doing this task is the essence of certainty.

A SCRIPT TO KICK-START YOUR CONFIDENCE

The ever-evolving recognition of one's own capabilities is the foundation of confidence. Your past experiences, worries, and frailties may have an effect on your assurance; nonetheless, you shouldn't let this deter you from moving forward. A powerless mental self image is the starting point for an absence of assurance. Find strategies to bolster the mental image of yourself that you have of yourself, and you will start to acquire a sense of assurance. People are drawn to those that exude confidence via the way they carry themselves, communicate, and interact with others.

Make a note of the things that are true about you, the things that are unique about you, and the wonderful things that others have said about you. Write them all down. It is not necessary for there to be a significant amount or importance. Nevertheless, it has to be authentic, positive, and distinct. Read through the Confidence launch script on a regular basis as well as any number of times you see necessary in order to assist yourself in remembering your positive qualities and accomplishments. It's possible that you're not giving proper credit to your successes and the good things that have happened to you, but that's not always the case. When good things start to occur in your life, be sure to include them into your writing as soon as possible. The development of your content will parallel the growth of your conviction. This will progressively reinforce your mental image of yourself and transform you from being skillful into being equipped and assured about yourself. Your behavior begins to shift in accordance with the beliefs that you have. Reading my self-assurance script, recording it on my phone, and listening to it a few times in the morning or whenever I feel like I need an extra boost is a technique that I have found to be beneficial. I also find that recording it on my phone and playing it back when I need a confidence boost is also effective.

What are the implications of this finding? In the event that you do not have trust in yourself, no one else will. Self-assurance is a skill, and just like any other competence, you may develop it more through time.

Enhancing Organizational Productivity Through Higher Emotional Intelligence In Corporations

In most cases, we make use of machines inside our organizational units. The robots lack any kind of emotional or intellectual capacity. This indicates that the efficiency associated to the 'electro-mechanical' elements of the organization or industry is measured and is restricted, in accordance with the standards given in the datasheet. The efficiency of artificial systems (machinery, software programs, and machine interfaces) is fixed, and it decreases with time; moreover, there is no flexibility for the development of efficiencies. We are able to establish maximal efficiency for artificial systems according to the configuration make-up of such systems. The electro-mechanical devices are not capable of exhibiting any emotional behavior. On the other hand, we have a variety of departments that manage the functionality of business flow. These departments include a wide range of people, each of whom has a unique degree of emotional intelligence. When personnel from different departments collaborate amicably and professionally while maintaining the emotional integrity of the business transaction or execution, they are able to do more with less effort, which leads to greater productivity. Wherever there are human beings involved, whether in the form of staff scattered across several departments or otherwise, there is the potential for total flexibility in improving efficiency. That indicates that the term 'emotional intelligence quotient' may be used to link employee productivity. Corporate manipulations may be conceived of in order to functionalize the efficiency based on the emotional and neurological framework of an employee's personality. This can be done in order to make the employee more productive.

From a psychological point of view: Emotional characteristics of every individual indicate his or her working state of mind; as a result, the productivity of that person may be inferred from those characteristics. When a person feels emotionally happy, both on an individual level and within the context of a team or department, his or her cognitive abilities improve (as a consequence of greater release of mood-boosting chemicals such as serotonin and oxytocin into the bloodstream), which ultimately leads to an improvement in productivity. On the other side, if the individual is disheartened, his or her ability for work production falls (due to increased release of the stress hormone cortisol into the circulation). As a consequence, the efficiency suffers. This idea of individual psychology may be coupled with team psychology or inter-departmental psychology to improve efficiency at various levels, which would ultimately lead to an increase in the profit margin of the corporation.

LESSON FOR THE CORPORATION It is essential that stringent standards be disseminated within "corporate employee circles" in order to prevent any financial damage to the company as a result of a lack of understanding of the idea and applications of emotional intelligence. In order to get the most out of emotionally intelligent workers and maximize their productivity, the company has to implement certain corrective measures and foster a healthy environment at work.

Knowledge, Authority, and Modeling are Important.

The terms "authority" and "leadership" are not interchangeable. The authority of the group's leader is something that, in many situations, can only be understood by those who are looking in from the outside of the group dynamic. The term "authority" often refers more accurately to a leader's "influence," and the degree to which a leader is respected by those they lead is proportional to the strength of the connections that leader maintains with those they lead. Therefore, those who hold positions of power can only be considered leaders if they are able to effectively influence the decisions and behaviors of others. When a team is effective, the leader is often seen as a fellow member of the team rather than as a superior. In times of transition, a leader seizes charge of the situation and guides their team through it, in contrast to the way an authority figure would drive their team through the transition. In conclusion, the threats of an authority person are not nearly as effective as the influence that may be exerted by an accomplished leader.

True leaders teach others by setting an example for others to follow, and they lead by accepting responsibility for themselves as well as their team. A leader has to have the experience and the expertise to be able to go ahead of their team, directing them towards the results they seek and through any tough moments that may arise. You should make sure that what you say and what you do are consistent with one another. You should avoid at all costs stating one thing while doing another since this will have a negative influence on how honest you are seen to be.

In the past, knowledge was power; however, this is no longer the case. We live in an era in which information is readily available, and as a result, it is undervalued and underutilized. We have access to an almost unimaginably large amount of information because of the internet; the important thing is how we put that knowledge to use. Creativity is the source of power in the contemporary day. The most accurate indicator of our specific levels of intellect is the manner in which we put our knowledge to work and apply it. We have the power to affect change in the world via creative thinking and logical observation, which are the foundations of both influence and innovation. Knowledge and experience provide the foundation for both. When we don't know something, our creative potential, the alternatives we have, the amount of impact we have, and our chances of being successful are all substantially diminished.

Exchange of information

In order to achieve success in any industry, you need to have some degree of communication skills. Having talents such as these enables us to better understand others around us and work together with them. Clear communication is extremely important in the corporate world or when we are leading a team since effective communication skills can considerably affect the outcome of negotiations in your favor. When it comes to the workplace, effective communication not only helps reduce errors and increases efficiency, but it also fosters trust and dependability among employees. It has been shown that improved communication in the workplace may boost employee morale and responsibility, particularly in situations where employees and team members are able to interact both horizontally across the chain of command and vertically up the chain of command. It may not be immediately visible, but improving your communication skills may also provide you with a significant number of financial rewards. To begin, we will discuss promotion and affiliate marketing; however, this topic will be expanded upon in a subsequent volume of the series.

Develop Relationships With Your Staff Members.

Building relationships is an essential component of every manager's job responsibilities. It must be an ongoing and proactive conduct that is, or eventually becomes, the very core of any manager's personal style. This is a must.

Because it is going to be difficult for our employees to embrace the change that we are implementing, the connections that we have with them are going to be put under pressure as a result. It is nearly always our fault because we are doing something to them that is going to have an effect, and we are causing it.

When there has been little to no effort put forward to cultivate major connections with the people who make up a team, it will be far more difficult to ensure that change is properly implemented.

This Is the Obstacle

It's not difficult to form new connections with people. It is challenging for many managers to carve out the appropriate amount of time to have meaningful talks with each and every member of their team. When this occurs, it is critical to take a careful look at the manner in which one spends their time and examine other approaches to their job.

There are occasions when managers are not sufficiently concentrated to guarantee that they fulfill their responsibilities. It is far simpler to take on duties that require less effort, which results in less time being made available for the people they serve.

Building relationships is at the center of a manager's purview as an activity set. It is not the job to move a pen about or operate with items; rather, the job is to manage people. The attention of any manager who is worthy of the term should always be on the people under their supervision.

How to Carry It Out

One easy action that can be taken to improve the quality of your relationships is to make it a daily goal to have one-on-one conversations with a certain number of the individuals in your life. Make it a priority to ensure that the manner you communicate with them conveys respect for them.

One simple method for doing this is to encourage the other person to do the majority of the talking by asking open-ended questions that are designed to elicit information from them. When that is the objective, it will be simple for you to let them speak while you perform the majority of the listening.

This may have a tremendous impact that demonstrates to them that you care about them as people and that you are willing to take the time to make them feel like an important part of the team.

You are only as powerful as your weakest member of the chain.

The title of this chapter comes from an article that was written in 1786 and published. These remarks are just as relevant now as they were over two centuries ago. This indicates that there are some strong ties, but there are also some weak ones, despite the fact that there are some strong links.

It's possible that some members of your team are blowing past their own personal bests and surpassing expectations. Despite this, it is possible that this will be eclipsed by someone whose low number of followers is preventing general advancement. In the next chapter, you will be provided with guidance and tactics on how to improve upon those areas of weakness.

It's possible that some of the problems are your own doing. We will walk you through the steps necessary to enhance them on your own. Let us get this party started.

Every member of the team is only as powerful as the team's weakest link.

Imagine that you are in charge of managing a baseball club. You are now on a winning streak and have a very excellent opportunity to go to the postseason. A more serious injury has been sustained by your team's top player than was first believed.

Despite the fact that he has been a vital cog in the machine that has been the team's success, you have no option but to put him on the bench. When you announce your choice and explain why you made it, the player raises objections.

"I'm good," he assures her. But you are aware that he is incorrect. You then proceed to explain to him why you are going to bench him and how playing him will really hinder the team's prospects rather than assist them.

You have the last word, and you are making every effort to ensure that things do not move in an undesirable direction. You, as the CEO of the company, may be required to make challenging choices in order to maintain the continuity of the chain. However, you may be of assistance by identifying the weakest connections and working to improve them.

The process of identifying the weakest link and determining how to address it

One further reason to monitor the development of your team is so that you can figure out who among them could be the weakest link. When monitoring the most critical indicators, you should pay attention to who is succeeding in completing their goals and who is falling short of those goals.

After the weak link has been discovered, it is essential to have a conversation about how to address it. Inquire with them about the possible issue that has arisen. Do they fail to meet their productivity goals because they are often sidetracked?

It's also possible that they've been in a grumpy mood as of late. Communicate with them in a manner that is discrete and does not cause a scene. While you are ensuring them that the discussion will remain confidential, you should request that they be open and honest with you.

While you go through this procedure, be sure to take notes. because it has the potential to motivate you to take action to help those people. If they exhibit symptoms of a more severe condition, such as burnout or mental anguish, you have a responsibility to provide them resources, including the assistance of trained professionals.

When it comes to providing assistance to a person who could be the weakest link in the chain, every choice matters. If they are easily distracted, you should encourage them to become less easily distracted. If it is required, study how they normally go about their business in order to spot any possible concerns.

Participate on the call as a listener, for instance, if your team communicates with clients over the phone. Create a mental list of your thoughts and observations. You may be able to locate the source of the problem based on the monitoring you've been doing.

After you have amassed a sufficient amount of proof, you will be able to design a plan to fortify and enhance the performance of that member of your team. Now, a weakness does not necessarily need to be associated with one's level of productivity. It's possible that someone on the team is trying to tear everyone apart.

There is a possibility that one of the members of your team has a poor demeanor and does not get along with the other members. It is possible that you may need to take the appropriate procedures, one of which is terminating their employment. Because the turmoil in the office is a distraction for everyone, it's possible that you won't have time to deal with it.

A person's negative attitude may also have an effect on the interactions they have with their customers. Because of this, there is a possibility that long-term clients would take their business elsewhere as a response to one or more unfavorable experiences they have had. And you certainly want to steer clear of this scenario.

What if you turn out to be the weakest link in the chain?

There are moments when you are the weakest link. If such is the situation, it is up to you to make the adjustments that are required. Take a look at the following suggestions for food for thought:

Take better care of yourself.

Not only is it vital for every member of your team, but it is also essential for you to practice self-care. The average day at the office may be quite chaotic and stressful. It is imperative that you and the members of your team put the health and safety of themselves and others first at all times.

Participating in mindfulness techniques, such as deep breathing, may help reduce stress. Determine the tasks that you will do each day. Find a nice balance between your job life and your personal life that works for you.

Get rid of the feeling that you're a fraud.

You might be under the impression that you attained your position of leadership by a random series of events. It's possible that you'll feel inadequate. It's possible that you won't feel like yourself at all.

Many outstanding leaders throughout history have suffered from the imposter syndrome at some point in their careers. It is natural for someone in your position to have these kinds of feelings. Make it a point to understand the warning signals, and often remind yourself that you are an effective leader who has the required qualities.

You have arrived at this point as a result of your hard labor, achievements, and abilities. Keep it in mind.

The Leader Who Is Able To Communicate

Effective communication is one of the most distinguishing characteristics of a leader, setting them apart from other members of the team in a significant way. People are more likely to pay attention to a speaker who is skilled with the English language, and they want the speaker's words to be understandable as well as succinct.

The communicative leader has the capacity to explain the objective in a manner that will cause everyone to nod their head in agreement with what they are trying to accomplish. Because of one's capacity to effectively handle communication among the members, problems that arise on the inside may be remedied quickly with little effort. On the other side, if the leader is unable to connect the dots between the objective and the team, then a plethora of difficulties are almost certain to arise.

Because of his or her capacity to effectively instruct team members, a leader who is good at communicating has the ability to transform an unproductive working atmosphere into one that fosters productivity. This leader also makes it a point to be accessible for consultation and to be able to listen intently to the thoughts and comments of those around them. At the end of the day, effective communication requires participation from both parties.

The Process of Becoming One:

If you want to be an effective communicative leader, you have to be able to regularly use the following methods in order to have positive interactions with your team:

Deal with it on a more intimate basis. In front of the team, you should try to avoid giving a lecture and instead focus on making the conversation more engaging. Always use a person's name when addressing them, and be sure to offer questions with open-ended answers so that individuals have the chance to react.

Don't become vague! Avoid using ambiguous language wherever possible, but particularly when providing directions and constructive comments. Be succinct, clear, and courteous in your communication to avoid confounding other people.

Foster a sense of compassion. The trap of hubris is one that many leaders fall into, and as a result, they wind up feeling that they are better than their contemporaries. However, the leader of the team is not the focal point of the group; he or she only fulfills a function within it. You, as the leader, are responsible for displaying empathy for the other members of the team by trying to put yourself in their shoes and imagining how you would react to the circumstances. You may be of more assistance to them in finding solutions to their challenges if you demonstrate empathy.

A communicative leader is someone who is able to choose the strategy that will work most effectively in any given circumstance. It is important to keep in mind that communication is also cultural; just because humor was successful with one individual does not indicate that it would be successful with another. It is important to be aware of the communication style of the other person and to adapt appropriately.

Intellectual Communication Is Essential.

When it comes to speaking not just with your contemporaries but also with the members of your team, it is essential to communicate with them in a way that shows respect and intelligence.

As a leader, one of your primary responsibilities should be to make sure that you are not the only one that learns and develops. You should assist your subordinates in learning how to get the most out of themselves as well as the circumstances in which they find themselves. When leaders inspire those they lead to be inventive and creative, it's possible that their followers may experience intellectual stimulation. It is crucial for you, as a leader, to assist your followers in developing the mindset that they are meant to do great things. They have the potential to achieve tremendous success if they put in a lot of effort, use their intelligence, and are enthusiastic about what they are doing.

How to encourage creative thinking and intellectual curiosity:

Here are some simple strategies to prevent your followers from being uninspired and ensure that everyone stays on the cutting edge of change. The most disastrous scenario would be one in which neither your employees nor the firm itself would advance in any way.

Put forth difficult tasks. Make it possible for your followers to demonstrate their skills and abilities by setting up scenarios in which they may do so. This may be accomplished via several techniques, including training, seminars, and sessions focusing on team development. Together, you will be able to participate in activities such as playing games and coming up with new ideas.

Inquire about things. One issue that might arise with some leaders is that they fail to consult their people by way of questioning. They are under the impression that they know everything, and as a result, nothing occurs. It is important to keep in mind that it is never inappropriate to seek the advice and assistance of others, even if you believe that you already have sufficient intelligence. Inquire about thoughts and comments from others. A good leader is someone who is able to take into consideration what others have to say and act accordingly.

cultivating a "I can do it" mentality and outlook. In the words of former President of the United States Barack Obama: "If they say we can't do it, we say, Yes We Can!" You have a responsibility to ensure that your workers are aware that, despite what others may think, the thing that matters most is that they believe they are capable of doing great things. have your agility, put in a lot of effort, and have a good mood while you're at work. Things are going to start looking good for all of you very soon.

Don't be too conformist about things. Do not be scared to attempt new things, and do not be afraid to push over the boundaries you have set for yourself. Imagine something completely different. If someone comes to you with a fantastic concept and you believe it has the potential to align with the values that your firm upholds, you should implement it. If someone suggests something to you that you haven't done before, don't be afraid to give it a go. Even if a member of the team suggests something that is completely absurd, it does not indicate that the idea cannot be successful. It is essential to have the ability to adapt easily in a changing environment. It's impossible to predict which ideas will be successful, but if you encourage your team to have the mindset that "no idea is a stupid idea," they'll feel more at ease contributing their ideas. If you continue to do the same things you always have, you won't be able to write new chapters in human history. Do not let your fear prevent you from taking chances.

Create an environment that encourages innovative thinking at work. Give your followers the freedom to put anything they want on their desks, as long as it is within reason and does not violate any laws, is unethical, or is in poor taste. Give them permission to decorate their workstations with whatever they choose, including collages, vision boards, their favorite phrases, or anything else they can think of. A office that is brightly colored and lively is always preferable than one that is dreary and gloomy. They will see you as more than simply a boss, but rather an inspiration, and as a result, they will have a greater enthusiasm for the job that they do.

Take a look. Acquire the skill of paying attention to what is going on in the world around you. This can assist you in generating thoughts on what may be done and how you should conduct yourself moving forward. Recognize that change is an unavoidable reality. The only way that people will be able to connect with you and what you have to give is if they believe that it will be beneficial to them in some manner. Demonstrate that you understand what it is that they need and desire.

Avoid working too hard. After you clock out for the day at your place of employment, if you go home and get a good night's sleep, you'll find that you're not only ready but also eager to head back to work the following day. You shouldn't put undue strain on either your followers or yourself, so don't let it happen. This is not an efficient use of the brain's capabilities. As a person's workload increases and their rest time decreases, the capacity of their brain begins to decrease. A mind that is capable of getting appropriate rest and being stimulated by their environment is a mind that is creative.

Employ the use of Vision Boards. You may create vision boards by using corkboards, which allow you to pin just about anything that comes to mind, including photographs of locations you wish to visit in the future, your vision for the future, or whatever it is that you're experiencing right now. If using Pinterest is more convenient for you, you may also utilize that website instead. Simply said, if you are able to picture something happening, then it is more likely to occur. If you are sincerely enthused by your goals, and if you believe that you can achieve them, then your brain will naturally work toward making them come true.

In addition to this, keep in mind that it is vital to acquire new knowledge on a daily basis. Never cease learning new things, such as getting to know new kinds of people and reading intriguing articles, books, and magazines. You will have a deeper understanding of the world you now inhabit by doing so.

A Program of Rewards

After evaluating their performance, competent managers should provide awards and incentives to workers. These should be given out after the employee assessments. This might be accomplished via the use of an appropriate incentives program that is run on a yearly basis. A incentives program is an excellent way to motivate staff to work hard. It helps individuals advance in their careers with a feeling of happiness and fulfillment, and it helps the organization boost its retention rate. Both of these benefits are mutually beneficial. The following are some suggestions for organizing a rewards program for your company.

The annual get-away.

Whether it is at the beginning of a well-known holiday break or at the conclusion of the company's fiscal year, a staff retreat should be held at least once per year. This might be a lavish event that involves the workers' families, but it would depend on the financial situation of the organization. It is also possible that it will take place in an unusual location. The retreat need to be an enjoyable time for the workers, and it ought to include activities like team-building exercises, a fancy dress competition, a children's performance, and a finale that consists of supper and dancing.

Honors and awards.

Awards should be given out to workers in recognition of their hard work. These awards might be given out in a variety of performance categories, such as "Best Salesman," "Outstanding Marketing Professional," "Best Production Manager," etc. Awards may also be handed out to acknowledge personnel not as "best," but rather as displaying development toward fulfilling organizational objectives. There is a possibility that some accolades may come with cash packages. Those who have shown exceptional performance may be awarded a comped trip to a popular tourist spot. There may be some exceptional achievers who are chosen to get a pay boost or a grade raise.

No matter what the nature of the award is, just acknowledging workers with a fitting prize offers the employee a psychological boost that their exceptional performance will be rewarded by upward advancement in the organization. This is true regardless of the type of the award.

The practice of.

Even while training is a tool for performance assessment, as was just said, it also has the potential to be a component of an awards program. If the training takes place away from the office, in an atmosphere that is both vacation and work, then the workers who were chosen to get the training will see it as an award and consider themselves fortunate to have received it. It is a great approach to reward workers and foster their development inside the firm to provide them with training in hill or sea resorts, or even at the company's headquarters located in other countries.

Note to reader: Negative reinforcement.

As a manager, it is inevitable that you will come across individuals who, despite the fact that they have been given chances to improve, continue to be non-performing liabilities. workers that have a disposition that is resistant to learning and growth tend to fall into this category, as do workers who are getting close to the retirement phase of their careers. These workers could be provided disincentives like an early retirement plan if they don't perform as expected. Employees who consistently demonstrate poor performance could be asked to leave their positions. It is necessary for a manager to anticipate the departure of such workers and to make preparations for their departure a significant amount of time in advance, in order to ensure that the employee's departure is as painless as possible.

The Fights Behind Closed Doors

The journey of every great leader begins inside themselves. They never reach to the point where they can lead others without first taking charge of their own life and overcoming the challenges that they face. They are aware of their shortcomings and draw on those flaws to improve themselves. The vast majority of leaders have encountered challenges and grown as a result, becoming far more capable than they were in the past.

First and foremost, a Servility Attitude

The best leaders are also excellent followers. They prioritize the needs of others over their own. The people are the priority of real leaders. They put the needs of others ahead of their own and do not worry about what they want. They have a fundamental belief that success does not come from the efforts of a single individual but rather from the collaboration of a group. A competent leader would never fail to acknowledge the contributions of the team members who worked on a successful project. Additionally, he or she is quite skilled at following directions. When a leader listens, they listen attentively and try to put themselves in the position of the individuals they are listening to.

When it comes to following directions, good leaders are meticulous and pay attention to the smallest of details. There are some individuals who have tried to be great leaders but have failed because they are unable to obey even the most basic instructions. The act of following is straightforward, yet not everyone is able to do it simply because they are unable to humble themselves. Simply demonstrating that you are following is a demonstration that you are not higher than everyone else in the room. If you possess this quality, then you have one of the most important attributes of a strong leader: the ability to inspire others.

Self-discipline is the second desirable quality.

Not only does self-discipline need restraint, but it also demands the ability to exercise one's own self-control and the bravery to turn down opportunities that involve matters of lesser significance. If you want to be a great leader, you have to be able to win private conflicts inside yourself before you can win wars in the public arena. This is the prerequisite for being successful in the public arena. You can't demand things of other people if you won't even do what you say you're going to do for yourself. When you become a leader, having self-discipline may take you a long way; for this reason, it is essential that you devote attention to developing it. The way that you carry yourself and the actions that you do may have an effect on the behavior of other people.

3. Drive or Enthusiasm

Everyone has to have a burning desire. They are able to accomplish anything, even if it seems impossible, because of the desire they have. The actions of great leaders are seldom taken just for the sake of taking action. They spend their time pursuing their passions. They almost always have a group of individuals on their squad that have the same level of enthusiasm as them. They are never at a loss for anything to strive for or an objective to accomplish. A good leader always has something that they aim to accomplish in the future. His enthusiasm extends well beyond the duties he must do and the responsibilities he must fulfill. It is the primary impetus behind everything he does and the energy that propels him forward.

Commitment, the fourth and final quality

It is imperative that you set a good example for your team if you want them to put in their best effort and generate great work. You need to be the example that they follow. Seeing the boss putting in the same amount of effort as the rest of the staff is one of the most effective ways to encourage employees. It is always encouraging to see your supervisor putting in effort to get the task done, rather than just barking orders at everyone else, since this demonstrates a greater level of commitment. You will not only gain the respect of your team but also instill the same devotion and enthusiasm in your employees if you demonstrate how devoted you are to achieving the objective of your team and your job as a leader by exhibiting how committed you are to doing so.

In addition to putting in a lot of effort, the best demonstration of dedication is not just accomplishing the task at hand but also keeping the commitments you make to others. You should fulfill your word whether you offered to throw a party on a Friday night or promised to pay an additional sum of money to your employees as a bonus. You don't only want to earn a name for yourself as a leader who puts in a lot of effort; you also want to be known for being fair. Once you have earned the respect of the whole team, it is more likely that they will offer the level of quality work that you have requested from them.

Responsibility Taking is the Fifth Essential Quality

A good leader is someone who accepts responsibility for their own acts and does not place blame on others for their own mistakes. If you want to be an effective leader, you need to be able to understand how to accept responsibility for your own actions. If you were unsuccessful in hitting the objective, rather than blaming others, look yourself to see where you went wrong. Instead of berating the whole team for the failed project, you should reflect on what went wrong and take the necessary steps to improve. You are mistaken if you believe that you have the right to wash your hands when things do not go according to the plans that you had made. You have the ability to lead your people to success, but you also have the potential to lead them to failure if you so choose.

) The Managerial Grid (The Managerial Grid)

The inability of the characteristics-based approach to discern effectively between qualities that may separate successful leaders from non-successful ones resulted in a change of focus away from traits and toward the behaviors of successful leaders.

Blake and Mouton (1978) highlight two distinct forms of leadership behavior: a) Concern for the people (also known as people-centered leadership), and b) Concern for production (also known as production-centered leadership). Both of these styles are stressed.

There are some parallels to be seen between the five management grids that they found and some of the leadership styles that were covered before. They are as follows:

1, 1Typology: This is a poor method of running a business. It is consistent with the leadership style known as laissez-faire, in which the leader does the least amount of effort necessary to get the task done. In this situation, the management does not care too much about either the employee or the output. A manager who uses this approach offers nothing in the way of leadership or direction to the people they supervise. He gives his subordinates more leeway to make decisions.

The 1, 9 management style, often known as the country-club management style, demonstrates how concern for output is balanced with a high one for the needs of workers or people. The manager who adopts this method demonstrates positive human relations while they are on the job. In his effort to gain social approval, he disregards the importance of being friendly.

The manager demonstrates an authoritarian leadership style known as the authority–obedience style. This is due to the fact that he is very concerned with productivity but is less concerned with the welfare of his staff. This category includes managers who are seen as "slave-drivers" in their places of employment. They are primarily concerned with attaining the output objective, and as a result, they push their subordinates beyond their capabilities. They have an irrational fear of falling short, and as a result, they use their power to make sure all of the deadlines are reached.

5, 5Style: This is referred to as the organization's men management. It is a style that is considered to be in the middle of the road and involves striking a careful balance between concerns for production and those of the employees. The manager and others want to make sure that the production goal is attained without embarrassing themselves in front of their coworkers.

9, 9 Style: This is a management style based on the concept of a team, often known as a democratic leadership style. The manager demonstrates a high level of care for both people and production in this aspect of the media organization; the editor and heads of unit who embrace it bring others along with them in their attempts to accomplish production objectives.

Blake and Mouton found that the 9, 9 style was the most preferred since it placed a high priority on both the people and the output. The contingency theory of leadership, on the other hand, contends that the perception that there is one leadership style that is essentially superior to others is inconsistent with the concept of leadership as a result of circumstances. This position, however, offers the basis for critique.

Baby Boomers and members of Generation Y are separated by a generational divide.

There are a variety of factors that contribute to the fact that there is now a generational chasm that separates Generation Y from their ancestral generations, in especially the Baby Boomers.

The Need for Human Contact

Millennials are known for their affinity for socializing and their enjoyment of working in groups and teams, in contrast to older generations such as Baby Boomers and Generation X, who are more at ease doing tasks on an individual basis. The latter believe that they get more work done when they work alone, whilst the former think that working in teams leads to greater brainstorming and an amazing interchange of ideas, which in turn produces newer, fresher, and better ways to approach accomplishing work.

The Reliance on Electronic Forms of Communication and Technology

Leigh Buchanon states in his book Meet the Millennials that members of Generation Y are masters of digital communication and significantly depend on cutting-edge technology in order to get all of their job done. This current generation came of age at an era in which the prevalence of the internet was expanding and knowledge could be accessed at any time. They did not have to spend hours poring through ancient newspapers, published journals, and books in order to locate information; instead, they could simply use Google, Wikipedia, or one of the many other search portals that were available to them.

On the other hand, members of the Baby Boom generation were raised at an era in which such innovations and conveniences were not readily accessible. They were used to doing in-depth research since they had to put a lot of effort into looking for objects and information in the past.

Millennials are excited and find it simple to work on topics that are unique and tough since knowledge is easily available to them. In addition, their creative talents enable them to search for simple solutions to any problem, which is one reason why they often explore for other routes to achieve their goals.

The Baby Boomer generation, on the other hand, went through a lot of hardship and had to put in a lot of work in order to achieve their objectives. This is maybe one of the reasons why they perceive the attitude used by Millennials to be juvenile and feel that giving a task one hundred percent of your effort is the only way to accomplish it correctly. Millennials are more likely to see this as the case.

They are of the belief that even if you need to spend hard work and time to achieve success, there are certain activities that can be excellently performed with less effort if you approach them in a creative way. This idea is definitely not popular with members of the Generation Y.

Enjoy Taking the Lead Role

Millennials are eager for their elders to comprehend their need for power, since they take great pleasure in taking command of various endeavors. In addition, if they provide an idea, they want to work on it; they strive to do things their way instead of always asking their baby boomer bosses for permission, authority, and agreement to do things their way. If you give them an idea, they want to work on it.

Tamara Erickson wrote an article that was published in the issue of Harvard Business Review that was dated February 2009, in which she stated that as a millennial, she expected to get the chance to pursue her ideas and fulfill them, and that she expected her superiors, many of whom were Baby Boomers, to understand that the working models have changed, and that they should therefore adjust smoothly to the new working style, which is the millennial style of working.

The Baby Boomer generation had a distinctive upbringing and was exposed to a distinctive range of circumstances; as a result, they find it challenging to accept and adapt to the manner in which Millennials do their job.

Need Constant Feedback

The Millennial workforce is very interested in receiving feedback on their performance. When they begin working on an assignment, they anticipate that their superiors will evaluate it in great detail and then communicate to them whether or not they have done a good job with it. Instead of just being critical of their performance, they want you to tell them how they may better if they have not performed up to the expectations.

In addition, members of Generation Y expect their Baby Boomer or Generation X superiors to be encouraging to them and provide prompt feedback on their work. However, baby boomers are not used to providing their workers with regular performance reviews and are not in the practice of showing appreciation for their staff members. This helps to explain why millennial employees often report feeling unsatisfied with their jobs when they are employed by Baby Boomer companies.

All of these factors make it quite evident why there is such a large generational difference between Baby Boomers and Millennials, and why the latter are unable to effectively lead the former.

Now that we've gotten that out of the way, let's talk about what employers and managers who are members of the Baby Boomer and Generation X generations need to do to revitalize their connection with Millennials and to lead them in the most effective manner possible.

Follow your dreams rather than the money.

To be a good leader, you need to have a clear idea of the goals you want to accomplish. I've lost count of the number of times I've seen somebody pursuing a promotion for the sole purpose of receiving a higher salary. You can't blame me if you think I'm mistaken about the significance of money in today's world, but it shouldn't be your primary motivation for seeking a promotion at work. Just for a moment, consider the reason for your increased compensation. You get paid more than the standard amount because it is expected of you to perform duties that go beyond what is outlined in your job description. This is why you receive additional compensation.

The action you should do is to write down what your vision is. This might include objectives that you wish to accomplish while you are in the position that you are currently in.

Put this objective into writing, along with a detailed action plan that includes stages that are simple to carry out. Make sure to write things down in the notebook that you always have with you. You don't have a notebook with you? Why shouldn't they?

The fifth lesson is that deeds are more persuasive than words.

This point is related to point number 2, and may go hand in hand with it. If you are pleased with the work that your workers have done, showing them your appreciation by providing them with time off or throwing a party for them is a great way to foster team building. This works a lot better than just expressing gratitude, although expressing gratitude is also a wonderful start in and of itself. Be the first person to take up a brush while cleaning up, and others will follow your lead. This is similar to principle number two, in which your actions will speak more loudly than words.

It could be a good idea to have a celebration for your workers to demonstrate your gratitude for all of the effort they've put in, and you should also make a point of walking around the office and thanking your staff members personally, as well as routinely praising them for their dedication to the task or job.

Take action and plan a get-together for your group.

Make an effort to express gratitude more often.

Flexibility in conduct, but not in values, is point number six.

This is an essential one for your own personal well-being. It is not necessary for you to always act as the upbeat and positive leader. Take a step back in some scenarios; go to lunch with some of the other workers; let your hair down at the company party; in short, shake things up a little. On the other hand, behaviors are not the same as values. The way you conduct your life is directly correlated to your values, and the following is a list of the basic principles that the British Army instilled in me:

• Bravery • Discipline • Respect for Others • Integrity • Loyalty • Selfless Commitment • Commitment to Something Greater Than Oneself

As you can see, these are the standards that you should always hold yourself to, no matter what. That is to say, you are free to spend your time at the company party having a drink and having a good time with your coworkers since this kind of conduct is acceptable. You have violated your own principles if you have ever laughed at the expense of another person or gotten so intoxicated that you made a fool of yourself.

Take action and jot down the values mentioned above, or come up with your own set of values and save them in an easily accessible location in the workplace. Make an effort to remember them, and behave appropriately.

Acquaint Yourself With The Ideal Methods Of Leadership

It is of the utmost importance that you educate yourself in the art of planning and strategy in this environment, which is always shifting. Why? Because if you don't, you won't really be able to be an effective leader, and it would be difficult to simply watch your aspirations evaporate into thin air if you don't do it.

Regrettably, not everyone is aware of the proper technique to plan a situation. You will, however, be in the fortunate position of gaining knowledge about the myriad of methods by which you may empower not just yourself but also the others in your immediate environment via strategic planning. This is how it is done:

Recognize that you are not perfect in every way. Do not be the sort of person that goes through life pretending to be flawless even when everyone knows that this is not the case. You will be able to take advantage of more lucrative and rewarding chances if you acknowledge both your own shortcomings and the fact that your company has a great deal of untapped potential. That is beneficial not only for you and your company, but also for the employees under your supervision. Consider your company's expansion as a top priority at all times.

Determine what went wrong in the past, what is happening right now, and what may be done in the future to prevent this from happening again. It will be difficult for you to handle your line of work as well as the people who are around you if you limit your concentration to just one time frame at a time. To avoid this difficulty, avoid focusing on just one time frame at a time. Find out what went wrong in the past or the errors that you have made in the past so that you will know what to do about it and so that over time, your company will develop to be the best that it can be. If you keep making the same errors, no one will trust you, which is bad not only for your company but also for your reputation. If you keep making the same mistakes, no one will trust you.

Concerning the state of your reputation, see to it that you maintain it. People are often saying that it is so difficult to develop a good reputation for oneself. In reality, it takes years, yet all it takes to destroy it is a few seconds' worth of carelessness, or maybe even just one error. These days, people aren't very forgiving; occasionally, they believe that just because you're in a leadership position does not imply that you are immune to making errors. You must keep in mind that being in a position of leadership comes with a great deal of responsibility. Because of this, it is imperative that you demonstrate to others that you are worthy of the opportunities that have been presented to you and that you have the ability to disprove the naysayers. And more than just proving your detractors wrong, it's crucial to take care of your reputation for yourself and for your company. If people can see that you are trustworthy, then your firm will be more successful, and you'll have possibilities to take on greater challenges in the future. This is why it's more important than ever to manage your reputation.

Surround yourself with exceptional people. When it comes to recruiting new employees, particularly those who will be reporting to you directly, you need to exercise extreme caution since you can't afford to have anybody but the most qualified professionals on your team. However, if things aren't going the way you planned the first time, try not to worry about it. There is no limit to the amount of improvement that may come from training these individuals. Activities and workshops geared at the development of cohesive teams serve this purpose. What is important is that you all strive toward improving things, and that you acknowledge there is a great deal more that each of you has to learn. Instead of hiring individuals who are comfortable with what they already know, you should look for candidates who are keen to learn new things.

Never undervalue the importance of having accurate data. You have a responsibility to be abreast of what is occurring in your immediate environment, and you must be aware of the significance of monitoring news broadcasts. Do not be the sort of leader who is unconcerned with the people he impacts or the customers he serves. It has nothing to do with being conceited or arrogant; rather, it has everything to do with being aware of who you are able to assist and what you can do to expand your sphere of influence.

A knowledge of technology is essential, or at least the ability to adapt. Take a moment to ground yourself in reality and acknowledge that you won't be able to get by with simply pen and paper at your side. discover how to utilize different sorts of modern technologies so that you may make your job simpler, and also discover other methods to educate yourself. Learn about what's new in the industry, then apply what you've learned to your area of work. It is always necessary to know how to ride change and move with the flow of life rather than being left behind, and one of the best ways to do this is to practice acceptance. If you have access to a sufficient quantity of resources, the load of work will be significantly reduced. Do your homework, and you'll be able to come up with some amazing ideas. Always be creative and original.

You, as a leader, have the ability to shape a prosperous future not just for yourself but also for your organization if you engage in strategic planning.

Adjust the Scope of Your Plan

If you have successfully enabled your team's Clarity of Action, shared Purpose, and Enthusiasm, now is the time to take a deep breath, step aside, and get out of your team's way so they can accomplish their goals. It is time for them to get moving and get things done. An motivated and well-informed workforce that is self-synchronized in their activities and understands who does what and when can give outcomes more quickly than a staff at Starbucks can offer a four-shot buzz. Prepare your leak-proof travel mugs, for these intrepid avengers are about to take flight!

On the other hand, if your project is complicated, the crew is dispersed across three time zones, and nobody knows anyone, then, well, let's just say that you will be the one who needs those four-shot buzz boosters.

Your communication process should be scaled according to the complexity of the project, the size of your core and extended teams, and any other relevant factors such as dedicated or shared resources, the physical proximity of team members, team members' previous experience working together, their levels of competency and expertise, and their performance history, as well as the cultural climate of the organization.

At the absolute least, you will want to make sure that every member of the team is aware of the date on which the deliverable must be handed in, their own portion of the work, the date by which it must be handed in, as well as the work and delivery dates of their colleagues. To put it another way, everyone has to have an understanding of the bigger picture, how they fit into it, who they rely on, and who relies on them, as well as who else is depending on them.

Katzenbach and Smith, in a thorough study of workgroups, identified the high-performance team as consisting of a limited number of individuals; having abilities that are complimentary to one another; being devoted to a single purpose, objective, and method; and holding themselves mutually responsible for the outcomes of their work.

The amount of communication effort needed to monitor and oversee a project or initiative will increase at a pace that is directly proportionate to the number of persons participating in the project as well as the actual geographical distance that separates them from one another. This is a terrible reality that you will have to face in every endeavor. I won't bore you with the study; rather, I want you to consider how much time you spend on an average project just to keep yourself informed and synced with the rest of the team. I've read studies that put the amount of time spent on email, meetings, phone calls, and person-to-person discussions at anything from two to six hours per person, per project, per week. In addition, almost everyone is working on many projects at the same time. Put in your own figures and figure it out on your own. How much hours do you spend each week on average speaking about each project? In a normal week, how many different projects do you have under way? You have my OK to have a pity party as long as you multiply the two numbers, deduct the product from the amount of hours you spend working each week (or the maximum you wish), and then multiply the result by two again. Even superheroes need some time to themselves every once in a while.

Now take into consideration how many individuals are on your team as well as the different communication channels that need to be used. There are two methods for individuals in teams consisting of only two people to communicate with one another: A to B and B to A. In the case of three-person teams, there are a total of six required pathways: A to B, A to C, B to A, B to C, C to A, and C to B. The formula for calculating the route is (N2 - N). There are twenty communication paths available if your core team comprises of five members (52 minus 5). By the time you've added one more partner to the mix, there will be 30 possible communication routes for the six of you. When you increase the size of the team to ten persons, you now have to deal with ninety different paths, and "nobody knows nuttin'!"

Every superhero has a nemesis who stands above all others. Ineffective communication is the devious, crafty, and unrelenting supervillain that project team leaders must fight against on a daily basis. Make sure that everyone is aware of WHO is doing WHAT and WHEN it has to be done, regardless of the scale or difficulty of your project.

Having A Clear Understanding Of Your Destiny

"Achieving your happiness is the only moral purpose of your life," and "that happiness," not pain or mindless self-indulgence, is the evidence of your moral integrity. Happiness, not pain or mindless self-indulgence, is the proof of your moral integrity, as it is both the proof and the effect of your dedication to the accomplishment of your ideals.

Rand, Ayn

Before utilizing the above phrase, I gave it some thought but ultimately decided against it since I questioned whether or not being joyful genuinely assisted someone in a leadership position. However, it did. People are unhappy when their values are in doubt or when things are not going particularly well in their lives. Leaders are leaders because they are content with the choices that they make, which are made for the good of everyone - rather than being focused on self. People are unhappy when their values are in question or when things are not going particularly well in their lives. If you are a badass leader, you probably already believe in your principles and have succeeded in living up to them. Consequently, there is a good probability that you are pretty pleased with the person that you have developed into. You may reach that degree of happiness via consistent physical activity that is guided by a clear sense of purpose. You have planned out the journey, so you are confident in who you are since you know where you are going and how to get there.

When one has a clear idea of where they are going and why, it is much easier to inspire others to follow in one's footsteps and strive toward the same goal. The value of having a sense of purpose is lauded to great heights in the book that was written by Jay Elliot, who once held the position of Senior Vice President of Apple. He gives an account of the manner in which Steve Jobs, who at first served as his guide and later progressively reversed the position, establishes a purpose for each and every product that Apple manufactures, so ensuring that the company's engineers and designers are aware of what it is that consumers are most likely to want. Steve Jobs has done a fantastic job of illuminating for people the significance of having a purpose in one's life in order to develop into a badass leader by presenting this impressive vision. If you are able to show others in the workforce the significance of the job that is being done, you will not only inspire them, but you will also spread excitement and belief. You receive the finest answers from your adverts for personnel because you lay out what the objective is right from the word "go."

One who goes about business with a sense of purpose is more likely to succeed than one who does not. A guy who has little faith in what he is doing is prone to cast suspicion on the objectives of his colleagues. Because he is unable to perceive the wider picture, it is possible that he may have feelings of insecurity and dissatisfaction with the task. He believes that the office cubicle in which he works is the center of the universe. Because it improves productivity and provides employees a sense of purpose, Japanese employers have, for many years, followed the practice of providing staff with an overview of the firm. They have a sense of pride for their accomplishments, despite the fact that they are rather little accomplishments in comparison to the bigger picture. The purpose is what gives them the desire to succeed, and this is something that is handed down through the chain, from management to staff, and from leader to management, since individuals without a purpose are less productive than they are capable of being.

When I was Richard Branson's employee, I recall reading an interview with one of his previous employees, and the guy was in awe of his former boss. He spoke about the amount of passion with which Branson approached each new initiative, and how his unwavering faith in the ability to succeed gave him his purpose. He also talked about how Branson was able to turn his ideas into reality. In addition to this, it inspired people who worked for him to create the highest quality work that they were capable of in order to be in line with the goal of the firm, which was to expand and flourish. Because he is an ideas guy, Richard Branson was able to alter his business to match the expectations of the market, which was something that stood out in this conversation. He was able to jot down thoughts and meticulously take notes on things that occurred to his mind, and all of these things contributed to his capacity to have purpose.

If you take a more macro view of how individuals live their lives, you'll see that one of the most significant motivators for day-to-day existence is really having a purpose. People who lack a sense of direction in their lives have a propensity to lead lives that are very routine and to question the meaning of life to such a degree that they become restricted and unable to connect to the world. The excellent examples of great leaders that we have had the privilege of seeing in our lives demonstrate to us that having PURPOSE is probably at the top of the list of behaviors that a leader has to have in order to ensure success in the conduct of company or in relations with other individuals.

Conversely, when you deal with individuals who have a muddled sense of purpose, they lack the clarity to know where the goalposts are and, as a result, they often fall short of really doing anything that is very notable. Imagine Bill Gates, when he hit his first roadblock, telling himself that he no longer had a purpose in life since the banks had turned down his request for a loan to start production because they didn't want to give him the money. If Bill Gates hadn't made that decision, our lives today would be quite different than they are now. He was clear about his goals and maintained a focused vision of them throughout the beginning stages of his journey, which ultimately led to his achievement of great success.

Your sense of direction and purpose has to be very clear. You need a mission statement or a justification for the things that you are doing in order to continue doing them. As soon as you have it, it makes the path much simpler to traverse, and there aren't nearly as many challenges along the way. When confronted with challenges, individuals who live their lives with a purpose are able to draw strength from those adversities to fuel creative solutions that take into consideration the fluidity of the market or the circumstances. That in no way precludes the possibility of development in your sense of purpose. It is possible for it to develop and expand when new possibilities arise; nonetheless, the original purpose should remain the primary focus point that assists a good leader in developing into a great leader.

www.ingramcontent.com/pod-product-compliance
Lightning Source LLC
Chambersburg PA
CBHW050233120526
44590CB00016B/2066